POISONOUS PLANTS

Also by Suzanne M. Coil

GEORGE WASHINGTON CARVER

FLORIDA

POISONOUS PLANTS

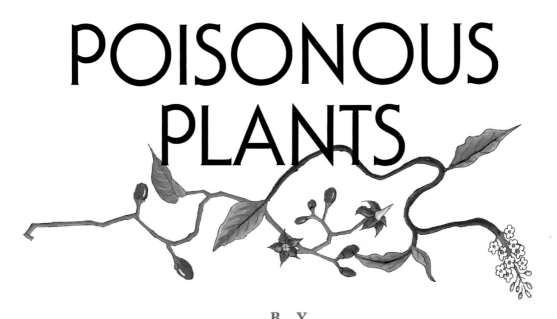

BY

SUZANNE M. COIL

ILLUSTRATED BY

ASTRID M. LENOX

A FIRST BOOK
FRANKLIN WATTS
NEW YORK/LONDON/TORONTO/SYDNEY/1991

Library of Congress Cataloging-in-Publication Data

Coil, Suzanne M.
Poisonous plants / by Suzanne M. Coil : illustrated by Astrid M.
Lenox.
p.   cm. — (A First book)
Includes bibliographical references and index.
Summary: Provides information on poisonous plants and their
identification, including both house plants and those that grow in
the wild.
ISBN 0-531-20017-5
1. Poisonous plants—Juvenile literature.   2. Poisonous plants—
Identification—Juvenile literature. [1. Poisonous plants.]
I. Lenox, Astrid M., ill.   II. Title.   III. Series.
QK100.A1C65   1991   90-13091   CIP   AC

FOR

*Mama, Ethel, Hildegard, and Astrid
in memory of the Rothengel Grössmutter,
who used the secret blessings
of plants to comfort and heal*

CONTENTS

GREEN POISON

One summer day, a little girl in Ohio decided to play house. On a toy dish, she arranged some pretty red berries she had picked from a shrub growing in the garden. A few hours after eating the pretend dinner, the girl died. Doctors learned too late that she had eaten berries from a poisonous daphne plant.

In Georgia, five children became ill after drinking some "tea" they had brewed from the leaves of a peach tree. Peaches, as you know, are delicious to eat. But other parts of the peach tree, especially the kernel inside the peach pit, contain one of the most dangerous poisons known.

When a toddler in Washington died suddenly, doctors thought that he had choked on a piece of candy until they discovered that he had eaten berries from a deadly nightshade bush.

Very few people die from eating poisonous plants, but each year many thousands of people are affected by them. If people knew more about plants, most of these accidents could be avoided.

Of the 30,000 species of plants that grow in the United States, about 700 are dangerous. Not every plant that threatens humans is deadly. Some are simply a nuisance. But other harmless-looking plants can cause pain, illness, and in rare cases, death.

Some dangerous plants contain poisons only in certain parts, while others are completely poisonous. But not all poisonous plants are bad. Some are used to make medicines.

Learn about the plants growing around you. This book will help you to recognize some of the most common poisonous plants.

You will notice that two names are given for every plant mentioned in this book. The first name given is the common name for the plant. The second name, enclosed in brackets, is the scientific name. (Spp. in the scientific name means "all members of the family.")

Some plants have several common names. Jimsonweed, for instance, is also called "thorn apple" and "Jamestown weed." But scientists all over the world call the plant *Datura stramonium.*

Sometimes several plants share the same common name. "Sumac," for instance, is a name used to describe several closely related plants, but only one of them, the *Toxicodendron vernix,* is poisonous.

Scientific names may look hard, but they prevent confusion. Every plant has its very own scientific name. It tells you exactly which plant is being talked about.

Learn to recognize the dangerous plants around you. Then you and your family can enjoy their beauty without being harmed!

PLANTS THAT MAKE YOU ITCH

If you ask your friends or family to name one poisonous plant, chances are they'll answer "poison ivy" or "poison oak." These common plants make six out of every ten Americans miserable at least once in their lives.

The gummy sap inside these plants contains a substance called urushiol. If a leaf or stem of the plant is damaged, the sap seeps out. If you touch the sap, it can cause your skin to turn red and feel as though it were burning. A little later, small blisters form and your skin itches fiercely. If you scratch the blisters, the rash may spread—and you run the risk of getting infections.

Urushiol is so strong that just a tiny droplet of sap contains enough to make hundreds of people miserable. You can spread the poison by touching other parts of your body with your hand. You can even get a rash without touching the plant itself! Petting a dog or cat who has walked through a patch, or touching clothes or objects that have been in contact with the plants can give you a nasty rash.

Poison sumac, like its close cousins, poison ivy and poison oak, also contains urushiol and can give you a miserable rash.

Learn to recognize these troublemakers and find out where they live in your neighborhood!

Poison Ivy [*Toxicodendron radicans*]

Poison ivy grows as a low plant or climbing vine along roadsides, in lightly shaded woods, on sand dunes, in parks, and in backyards. The leaves are formed of three separate parts called leaflets. The leaflets may be shaped like mittens, with one or more lobes. Sometimes they have smooth edges and sometimes they have small "teeth" along

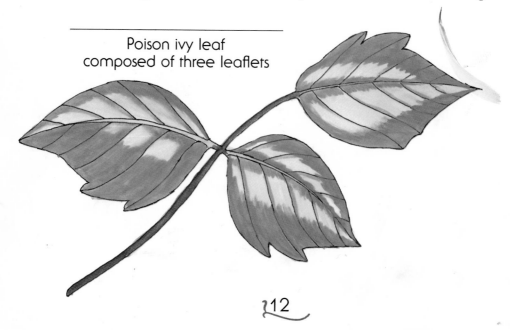

Poison ivy leaf
composed of three leaflets

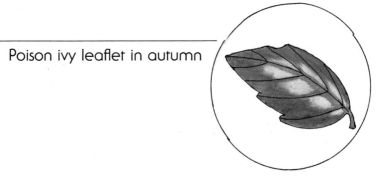

Poison ivy leaflet in autumn

the edges. The plant has small, greenish white flowers followed by small, yellowish berrylike fruits that hang in clusters. In autumn, the leaves turn bright red, gold, and orange.

Poison Oak [*Toxicodendron diversilobum*
grows on the West Coast];
[*Toxicodendron toxicarium* grows in the Southeast]

Poison oak often grows near poison ivy. Eastern poison oak
looks a lot like poison ivy, but the undersides of its leaves

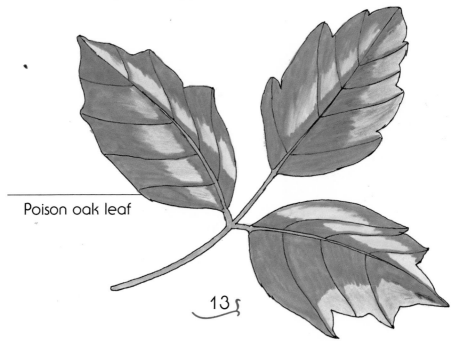

Poison oak leaf

13

are covered with soft, velvety hairs. Western poison oak also looks like poison ivy, but its leaflets are larger. Poison oak has small, greenish yellow flowers that develop into small cream-colored fruits similar to those of poison ivy. The leaves turn deep red in autumn.

Poison Sumac [*Toxicodendron vernix*]

Shaped like a small tree or shrub, poison sumac grows near streams and in swamps and marshes in the eastern United

Poison sumac leaf
composed of nine leaflets

States. Its leaves are composed of between five and thirteen leaflets. Poison sumac has stalks of small whitish flowers that later form clusters of round whitish fruits. Nonpoisonous sumacs have red fruits. In autumn, poison sumac leaves turn bright red.

If you're unlucky enough to develop a rash from touching these plants, you can buy a lotion or ointment to relieve the itching at your local drugstore. If you have a severe rash, you should see a doctor.

Caution: *Never* burn poison ivy, poison oak, or poison sumac plants to get rid of them. Burning releases tiny droplets of sap into the air. They can get into your eyes and lungs, causing severe problems.

CHAPTER 3

PRETTY POISON GARDENS

Everyone in town admires the pretty house with the lovely garden. In springtime, azaleas, rhododendrons, daffodils, and hyacinths burst into bloom. Morning glories, daphne, and dark green yew bushes grow nearby. Lily-of-the-valley flourishes in the shade of the oak and horse chestnut trees. In summer, the oleander bush is covered with red flowers, a castor bean plant covers a bare corner, and beds of fox-glove and delphinium send up spikes of lovely flowers. In late fall, autumn crocuses bloom. The family who live in the house enjoy their garden—but they probably don't know that almost every plant in it is poisonous!

If you live near a garden or park, you've probably seen many of these poisonous plants!

Daffodil [*Narcissus pseudo-narcissus*]

The cheerful daffodil is one of the first flowers to bloom in

Daffodils

17

spring. Daffodils are easy to recognize by their trumpet-shaped flowers; their bright, sunny yellow color; and their long, flat leaves. Daffodils are grown from bulbs that look very much like onions. But eating the plant, especially the bulb, is dangerous. Just a small bite of the bulb can make you very sick. Jonquils [Narcissus jonquilla] and narcissus [Narcissus poeticus] are close relatives of the daffodil—and these bulbs are equally poisonous.

Hyacinth [*Hyacinthus orientalis*]

Another springtime favorite is the fragrant hyacinth. The flowers are formed of tight clusters along a spike, and come in every color of the rainbow from pure white to deep purple. Narrow, flat leaves grow upward from the base of the plant. Hyacinths grow from large bulbs that resemble onions. The bulbs are poisonous. Eating just a small amount of a hyacinth bulb can cause a severe stomach upset.

Hyacinths

19

Lily-of-the-valley

Lily-of-the-Valley [*Convallaria majalis*]

The small lily-of-the-valley is beloved for its delicate sprays of white or pink bell-like flowers, its canoe-shaped leaves, and its lovely scent. You'll find patches of it growing happily in shady places and in garden borders. Hundreds of years ago, people believed that if a potion made from the flowers was rubbed on someone's forehead, it would make that person have "good common sense." But common sense says "don't fool around with lily-of-the-valley." The entire plant (especially the tiny fruit) contains a poison so strong that four drops of it can kill a dog.

Yew [*Taxus* spp.]

There are many members of the yew family, and they are found all over the United States. These attractive shrubs and trees are often planted near houses. Their shiny dark leaves stay green throughout the year. The fruit is a soft, bright red, cup-shaped berry that contains one brownish black seed. The seed is deadly. People have died within minutes after eating yew seeds.

Rhododendron, Azalea [*Rhododendron* spp.]

The large evergreen shrubs that we call azaleas and rhododendrons are grown in the coastal and mountainous regions of the United States. In springtime, they burst into bloom with dazzling clusters of white, orange, pink, red, and purple flowers. All parts of these plants are dangerous, especially the flowers and leaves. Nibbling on a leaf can make you very sick. Eating honey made from the flowers can also make you ill.

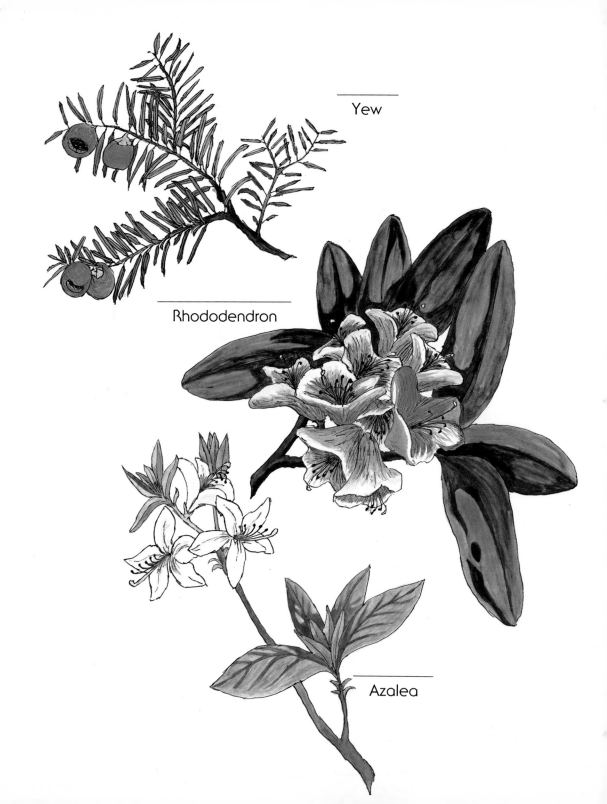

Yew

Rhododendron

Azalea

Not *all* members of the rhododendron family are dangerous. Some harmless—and tasty—relatives are huckleberries, blueberries, and cranberries.

Oleander [*Nerium oleander*]

The pretty oleander is a popular outdoor shrub in southern and Pacific coast states. It is sold as a houseplant in northern states. The oleander has lovely, fragrant flowers that range in color from white to dark red. The dark green leaf has a prominent rib on the underside. All parts of the oleander are very dangerous. Honey made from oleander blossom nectar is poisonous. Never burn oleander branches in the fire at a cookout. Never use an oleander twig to hold a hot dog or marshmallow over the fire. People have been poisoned by eating meat cooked over burning oleander branches. Even the smoke can make you sick.

Oleander

In spring,
blossoms cover Daphne branches.
They are followed by leaves and berries (right).

Daphne

Daphne [*Daphne mezereum*]

Found in gardens all over the United States, this small beautiful shrub blooms in the springtime before its leaves come out. The branches are covered with sweet-smelling clusters of small, four-lobed flowers in colors ranging from pale pink to rosy purple. After the flowers die, daphne produces small seeds that look like bright scarlet beads. All parts of the plant are extremely dangerous, especially the seeds, bark, and leaves. A few seeds are enough to kill a child.

Morning Glory [*Ipomoea purpurea*]

The common morning glory vine, with its familiar white, pink, or blue flowers and heart-shaped leaves, grows every-

Morning glory seed

Morning glory

where. Its funnel-shaped flowers open in the morning and last for only a few hours. The seeds of the morning glory are shaped like lentils and are very dangerous. Eating them can cause severe mental problems and brain damage.

Castor Bean [*Ricinus communis*]

The castor bean plant, which looks like a small tree with green, reddish, or purplish branches, grows everywhere. Its large clusters of flowers produce spiny pods, each containing three shiny, beautifully spotted seeds. These seeds are extremely poisonous. Two seeds can kill a child; six seeds

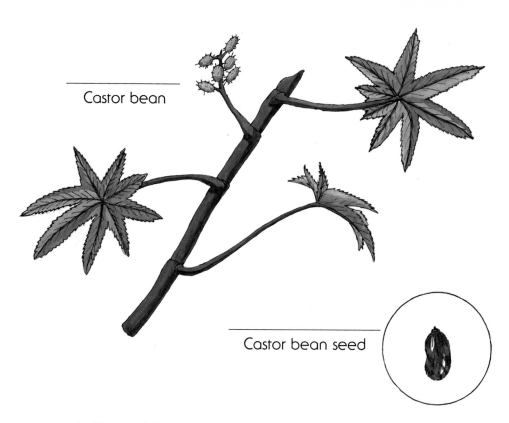

Castor bean

Castor bean seed

can kill an adult. In Mexico, necklaces made from castor bean seeds are sold to tourists. Never chew or suck on strings of beads. They might be castor beans.

Foxglove [*Digitalis purpurea*]

Found all over the United States, the handsome foxglove is an important, lifesaving plant. It is the source of digitalis, a drug used to treat heart disease. The large, hairy leaves stay green all winter. In summer, the plant sends up tall columns of thickly clustered, bell-shaped blossoms. The lavender or purple flowers often have little spots inside. Although foxglove has saved many lives, its flowers, leaves, and seeds are very dangerous and should never be eaten.

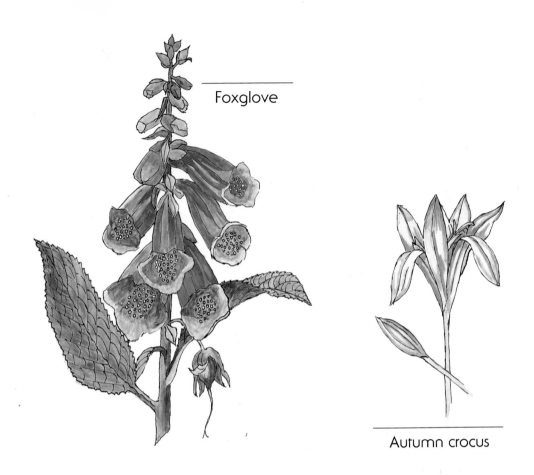

Foxglove

Autumn crocus

Autumn Crocus [*Colchicum autumnale*]

The ancient Greeks and Romans used the poison in this plant as a medicine. Now it grows all over the United States and is one of the last plants to bloom before winter comes. The white or bright pink flowers appear in autumn after the leaves of the plant have died. All parts of the plant, especially the seeds and the bulb, are dangerous. People have been poisoned from drinking milk from cows, sheep, and goats that have eaten autumn crocus leaves and flowers.

Delphinium, Larkspur [*Delphinium* spp.]

More than 250 members of the delphinium and larkspur family grow across the United States, and all of them are dangerous. The leaves of the plant cluster near the ground. In summer, tall, narrow spikes shoot up and are covered with white, yellow, red, rose, or blue flowers. Each flower has a small "spur" at its base. Eating the leaves and seeds of these plants can cause paralysis or death.

Delphinium

Oak leaves and acorns

Oak [*Quercus* spp.]

Many kinds of oak trees grow all over the United States. These stately giants are among our most treasured trees. Their leaves vary in size and shape, but all oak trees produce acorns. Unfortunately, the leaves and acorns of many kinds of oak trees contain a harmful poison. American Indians used to boil acorns several times to get rid of the poison. Then they would grind the acorns into meal to make a kind of bread. But be safe—never, never chew on any acorns.

Horse Chestnut, Buckeye [*Aesculus* spp.]

These majestic trees grow all over the United States. In springtime, cone-shaped bouquets of white, yellow, pink, or red blossoms stand up like candles along the branches. In the fall, the trees produce large, smooth, round seeds. These beautiful seeds, which look like polished wood, are surrounded by spiny, green husks. The seeds are fun to collect, but beware! These "buckeyes" or "chestnuts"— along with the leaves of the tree—contain a poison that, if eaten, can make you sick.

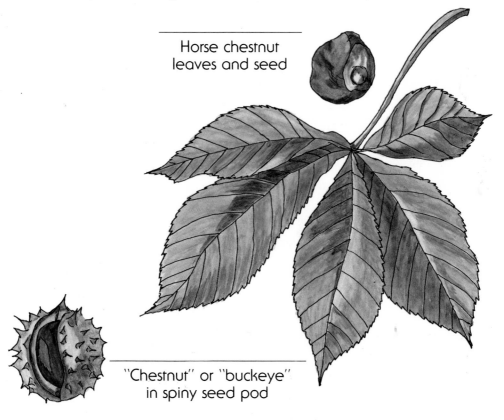

Horse chestnut
leaves and seed

"Chestnut" or "buckeye"
in spiny seed pod

PERIL IN WILD PLACES

Summertime is camping time, and exploring the wilderness can be lots of fun. As you hike through woods and fields, you'll encounter many unfamiliar plants, including some poisonous ones. Some of them have fruits and berries that look good enough to eat, while others resemble perfectly innocent plants. Avoid trouble outdoors by learning to recognize these interesting wild plants.

**Climbing Nightshade
(also called Bittersweet Nightshade)
[*Solanum dulcamara*]**

Often found in fields, parks, and vacant lots, this attractive vine usually climbs around other plants. The pretty purple or white flowers have five petals that turn back to show a bright yellow cone in the center. The nightshade's orange-red berries look like small cherry tomatoes. But unlike tomatoes, the nightshade's berries are poisonous and can cause serious problems if eaten.

Climbing nightshade

Death Camas (also called Black Snakeroot)
[*Zigadenus* spp.]

Its name alone tells you that this plant is dangerous. About
fifteen kinds of camas plants are found growing in meadows, pastures, gardens, and open areas across the United
States. The camas has long, narrow grasslike leaves and

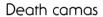

Death camas

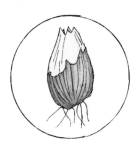

Death camas bulbs
are easily mistaken for onions.

tiny pink, white, or yellow flowers. It is easy to mistake a camas plant for a wild onion because it grows from a bulb that looks just like a small onion. But the camas bulb does not smell like an onion. Many cattle have died from eating this innocent-looking plant.

Jimsonweed (also called Thorn Apple, Jamestown Weed, Stinkweed) [*Datura stramonium*]

Jimsonweed likes to grow in dry, sandy soil, near pine woods, and even in vacant lots in cities across the United States. It resembles a little tree, with a thick stem and many branches. The leaves are green or purple, and give off a very bad smell. The five-pointed, trumpet-shaped flowers are white or pale violet. They point upright on their stems. The hard, thorny fruits (called "thorn apples") contain many seeds. The seeds are extremely poisonous. The plant got its name when, in 1676, some people in the Jamestown colony in Virginia became mentally unbalanced for several days after mistakenly cooking and eating young Jimsonweed plants.

Jimsonweed.
Notice the "thorn apple" fruits.

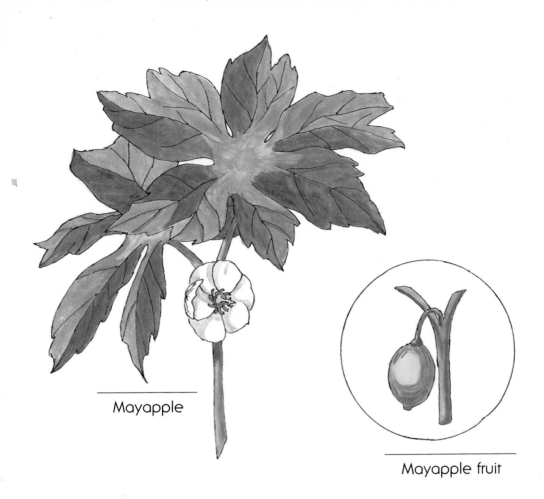

Mayapple

Mayapple fruit

Mayapple [*Podophyllum peltatum*]

A resident of damp meadows, pastures, and woodlands all over the United States, this plant is easily recognized by its large, umbrella-shaped leaves. The fruit of the mayapple looks like a small lime until it ripens and turns lemon yellow. All parts of the mayapple plant contain poison. Stay safe! Don't be tempted to sample the tasty-looking fruit of the mayapple.

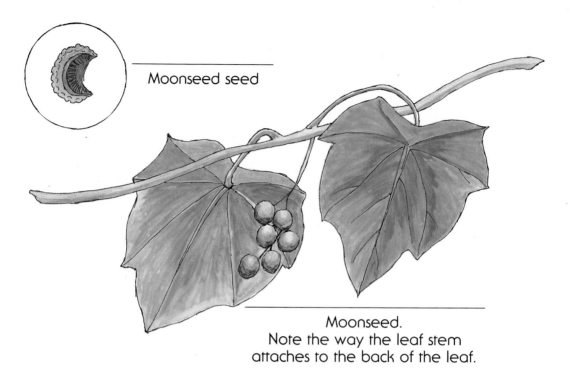

Moonseed seed

Moonseed.
Note the way the leaf stem
attaches to the back of the leaf.

Moonseed [*Menispermum canadense*]

Moonseed vines grow in moist woodlands throughout the central and eastern United States. Moonseed looks similar to a grapevine. Here are several ways you can tell them apart. Moonseed leaves are shaped like grape leaves, but are smooth underneath, while grape leaves have hairy undersides. Moonseed leaves have smooth edges, while grape leaves have little "teeth." Moonseed leaves are attached to their stalks differently. (See illustration.) Moonseed fruits look just like small bluish black grapes. But, unlike grapes, the fruits contain only one crescent-shaped seed. The fruits are extremely dangerous. People who thought they were eating wild grapes have died from eating the fruits and seeds of this plant.

Poison Hemlock
(also called Fool's Parsley)
[*Conium maculatum*]

This innocent-looking plant grows in waste places and gardens all over the United States. Its dark green, fernlike leaves grow on hollow stems, and its small, dull white flowers form in tight clusters. The tiny seeds are flat and oval-shaped, and smell like licorice. The root of the plant resembles a parsnip. This dangerous cousin of carrots, celery, parsnips, and parsley is extremely poisonous. Indians used to dip their arrows in the poison from this plant. When Socrates, the ancient Greek philosopher, was sentenced to death, he was given a cup of poison hemlock tea to drink.

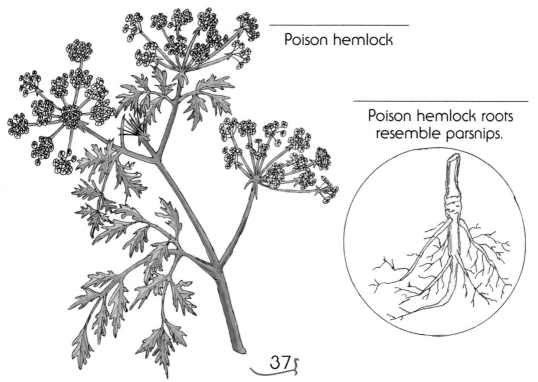

Poison hemlock

Poison hemlock roots resemble parsnips.

37

Pokeweed [*Phytolacca americana*]

A native of the mainland United States and Hawaii, pokeweed likes to grow in wet, rich soil. It is found in fields, on roadsides, and near buildings and barns. The long leaves of this shrublike plant have red veins and grow on sturdy purplish green stems. The white flowers form in large, droopy clusters. The shiny, purplish black fruits are a little larger than blueberries. Pokeweed can grow up to 10 feet (3m) high, and the larger the plant grows, the more dangerous it becomes. All parts of this plant are poisonous, especially the roots. Some people cook the leaves and make pie with the berries. Cooking the leaves and berries makes them edible, but eating them raw can be dangerous.

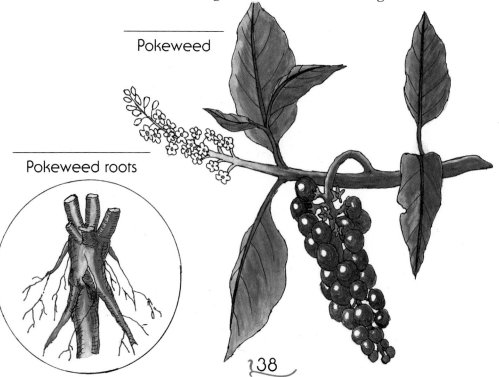

Pokeweed

Pokeweed roots

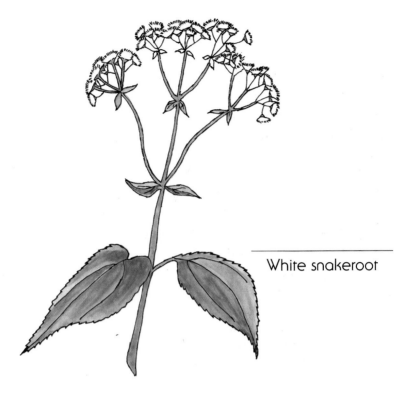

White snakeroot

White Snakeroot [*Eupatorium rugosum*]

This plant grows in damp areas, open woodlands, and near streams in the central and eastern United States. Its leaves have three distinct veins, and its tiny white flowers cluster in flat heads. The small seeds are flat and have "hairs" at one end. All parts of this plant are poisonous. In the eighteenth and nineteenth centuries, many people died from an illness called "milk sickness." Milk sickness was caused by drinking milk that came from cows who had eaten white snakeroot plants. Some historians say that Abraham Lincoln's mother died of milk sickness. It was one of the most common causes of death among early settlers.

Yellow jessamine

Yellow Jessamine (also called Carolina Jessamine)
[*Gelsemium sempervirens*]

This lovely evergreen vine grows in fields and woods from Virginia to Texas. It is also sold as a houseplant. Its glossy, dark green leaves and sweet-scented, tube-shaped yellow blossoms are so beautiful that it is hard to believe that yellow jessamine is dangerous. But all parts of the plant are poisonous. People have gotten sick from eating honey made from the nectar of the blossoms. Cattle have died from eating the leaves of this plant.

Wild Mushrooms

Wild mushrooms pop up from late spring through fall. They are found in forests, near rotting stumps and logs, in meadows, and on lawns. Some wild mushrooms, such as the fly agaric, look as poisonous as they are. Other poisonous mushrooms, such as death cap, death's angel, and destroying angel, look perfectly harmless, but they can kill you. Not all wild mushrooms are poisonous. But it is very difficult, even for experts, to tell the difference between poisonous mushrooms and mushrooms that can be eaten. **Be safe:** *Never, never eat wild mushrooms.*

Poisonous mushrooms

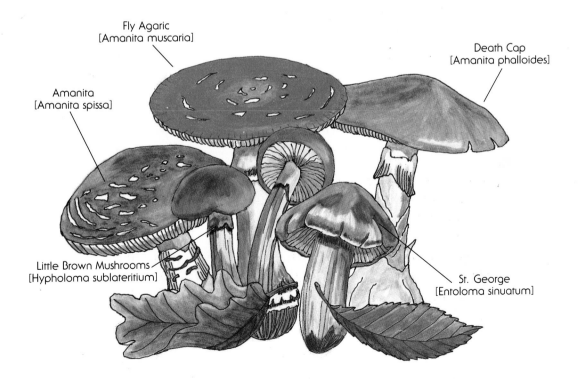

Fly Agaric
[Amanita muscaria]

Death Cap
[Amanita phalloides]

Amanita
[Amanita spissa]

Little Brown Mushrooms
[Hypholoma sublateritium]

St. George
[Entoloma sinuatum]

NOT-SO-HARMLESS HOUSE PLANTS

Indoor plants are becoming increasingly popular. Not only do they add beauty to our homes, offices, and other buildings, they also serve as natural air-pollution control systems. Leafy plants clean the air of harmful fumes that are sometimes given off by modern building materials, carpeting, and furniture. Even though they help to keep our air clean, some common house plants can cause trouble. It's wise to keep these particular plants away from small children and pets.

Caladium [*Caladium* spp.]

There are more than a dozen kinds of caladium. These lovely plants grow up to 4 feet (1.2m) high. Their beautiful, large, arrow-shaped leaves are thin, almost transparent, and come in many colors. Some are plain green, while others are banded or spotted with white, silver, pink, rose, or red. Eating or nibbling on the leaves can cause severe stomach pains and burning and swelling of your mouth and throat.

Jerusalem Cherry [*Solanum pseudo-capsicum*]

The pretty Jerusalem cherry plant grows up to 4 feet (1.2m) tall indoors. It has shiny dark green, oblong leaves and small white flowers that grow in clusters. Most attractive of all are the plant's small, bright red or yellow berries that resemble little tomatoes. All parts of the plant are poisonous, but the berries are especially dangerous. Ten berries contain enough poison to kill a child.

Caladium

Jerusalem cherry

Dieffenbachia

Dieffenbachia (also called Dumbcane) [*Dieffenbachia* spp.]

Dieffenbachia is one of the most popular indoor plants. It grows up to 6 feet (1.8m) tall and has large leaves that vary in color from dark green and yellowish green to pale green and white. Biting the leaves can cause your lips, mouth, and throat to burn and swell painfully.

Philodendron [*Philodendron* spp.]

If you have only one plant in your home, chances are it is a philodendron. This pleasant vine is the most common house plant. It adapts itself to all sorts of indoor conditions and grows easily even in dark corners. Its heart-shaped leaves range in color from light green to dark green, but they are very poisonous. A child or pet can die from eating only one leaf.

Philodendron

HOLIDAY HAZARDS

Potted plants make welcome gifts for holidays and special occasions such as birthdays and anniversaries. Plants are also sent to cheer people who are sick or in the hospital. At Easter, people often give one another azaleas, daffodils, narcissus, jonquils, and hyacinths. You know from what you've read previously in this book that all of these plants are poisonous. But do you know that some of the plants we use to decorate our homes at holiday time are also dangerous?

English Ivy [*Hedera helix*]

English ivy is a lovely evergreen vine. It covers the outside of houses and buildings and is used as a ground cover in shady places where grass will not grow. It is also a common house plant. English ivy's dark green leaves and pea-sized black berries are a familiar sight, but they contain a poison that can make you sick. Since ancient times, people have

English ivy

English ivy berries

brought English ivy into their homes to celebrate their winter festivals. Enjoy this plant at holiday time, but keep it away from small children and pets.

Holly [*Ilex* spp.]

Many kinds of holly bushes and trees grow all over the United States. At Christmas, people use holly branches for decoration. Sprigs of holly are often pictured on greeting cards and gift wrapping. These beautiful evergreen plants are easily recognized by their waxy, lustrous, dark green leaves and their cheerful red berries. Although the leaves, which are hard and thick, have small spines that can prick your skin, it is the berries that are dangerous. They contain a strong poison that can cause serious problems if eaten.

Mistletoe [*Phoradendron* spp.]

Mistletoe is a parasitic plant. This means that it gets its nourishment from other plants. It grows on hardwood trees, especially oak trees. Mistletoe has pale green, leathery leaves; tiny green flowers; and fleshy white berries. All parts of the plant are poisonous. At Christmas, people hang sprigs of mistletoe over doorways. Custom says that anyone caught standing under the mistletoe can be kissed!

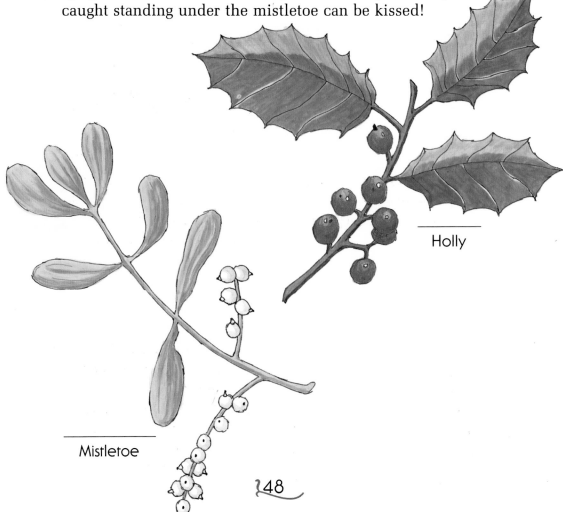

Holly

Mistletoe

48

DANGER ON THE DINNER TABLE

The next time you go to a supermarket, take a look at the tempting displays in the produce section. Could poisonous plants be lurking among those neat piles of fresh fruits and vegetables? Believe it or not, the answer is *yes*! Some of our most common fruits and vegetables can be dangerous if they are not prepared or cooked properly.

Rhubarb

Rhubarb has been called the most dangerous plant in the garden. The long, red stems of the plant can be eaten cooked and make a delicious pie. But the green parts of rhubarb, especially the large, attractive leaves, are extremely dangerous. A small bite of a leaf can cause painful poisoning. Eating a larger amount of the leaves can kill you.

Rhubarb

50

Potato (White or Irish Potato)

Potatoes—french fried, baked, or fixed in other ways—are one of our most popular foods. But did you know that the ordinary white potato is a cousin of the deadly nightshade? The potato plant grows as a sprawling vine. The leaves, stems, and other green parts of the plant contain a deadly poison. When you peel potatoes, make sure you cut away any parts that look green and remove any sprouts growing out of the potatoes. The sprouts are especially dangerous. Cooking does not destroy the poison found in the green parts of potatoes.

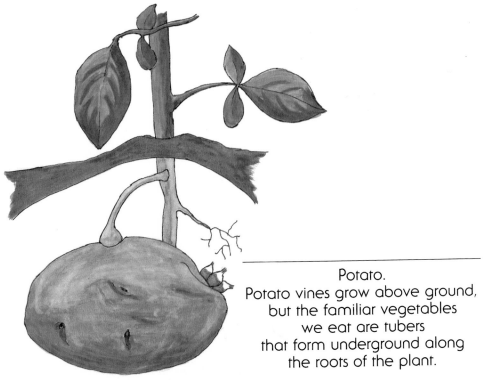

Potato.
Potato vines grow above ground, but the familiar vegetables we eat are tubers that form underground along the roots of the plant.

51

Tomato

Tomato

For many centuries, people thought tomatoes were poisonous and raised these attractive vines only to decorate their gardens. Now we know that tomatoes themselves are good to eat. But the leaves and vines of the tomato plant really do contain a poison that can cause serious problems if eaten.

Apples, Cherries, Apricots, Peaches, and Plums

Apples, along with cherries, apricots, peaches, and plums, are among the most delicious fruits in the world. Eat as many of these wonderful fruits as you like, but don't eat the seeds. The pips of apples and the kernels inside the pits of cherries, apricots, peaches, and plums all contain cyanide, one of the deadliest poisons known.

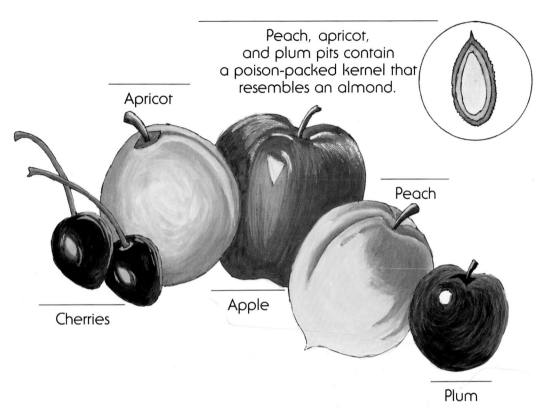

Peach, apricot, and plum pits contain a poison-packed kernel that resembles an almond.

Apricot

Peach

Cherries

Apple

Plum

Beans

Sometimes a food can be perfectly safe if it is cooked, but dangerous if it is eaten raw. That's the case with beans. Kidney beans, pole beans, runner beans, lentils, and other kinds of beans are common ingredients in many tasty dishes. But beans also contain poison. Fortunately, the poison breaks down in the cooking process. To stay safe, always cook beans before eating them. Don't eat raw beans, especially lima beans. Lima beans contain large amounts of poison, and eating even a few raw lima beans can make you sick.

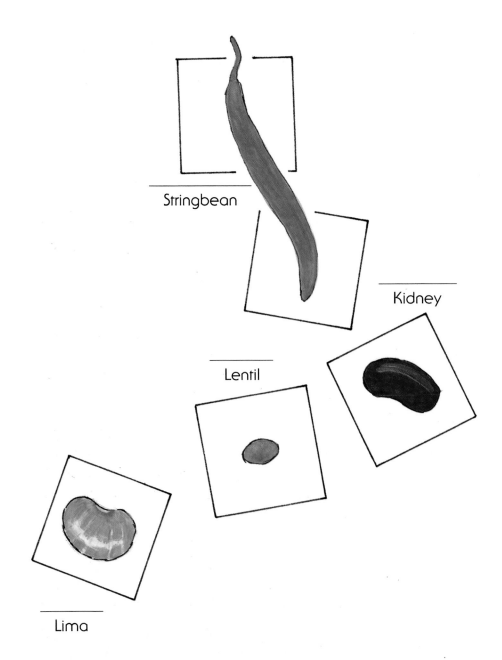

Stringbean

Kidney

Lentil

Lima

SOME COMMONSENSE RULES

Throughout this book, you have learned about some of our most poisonous plants. Fortunately, only a few of the nearly 700 poisonous plants that grow in the United States are extremely dangerous. But even mildly poisonous plants can cause lots of trouble.

Your best defense against plant poisoning is to not let it happen. You can do this by learning the names of poisonous plants, what they look like, and where they grow. If you follow these commonsense rules, you can prevent illness and tragedy.

1. Know which plants in your house and garden are poisonous.
2. Never put any plant or plant part in your mouth unless it is commonly used for food. (Some plants commonly used for food must be cooked first.)

3. Don't chew or nibble on the leaves, flowers, twigs, or stems of unfamiliar plants.
4. Don't eat any unknown berries, even if you see birds or other wildlife eating them. The berries that wild birds and animals eat are not always safe for humans.
5. Don't eat the seeds of any plant unless they are commonly used as food. (Some of these seeds may need to be cooked first.)
6. Don't eat the bulbs, roots, or tubers of unknown plants, especially if they look like onions.
7. Don't eat wild mushrooms. Eat only mushrooms that were bought at the supermarket.
8. Don't eat or touch plants that ooze colored or milky juice.
9. Don't burn unknown plants. Don't use unknown twigs to roast hot dogs or marshmallows over your campfire. Don't cook food over fires containing the branches and leaves of unknown plants.
10. Don't leave dangerous house or garden plants where small children or pets can reach them. If there are little children in your family, get rid of all your dangerous plants.
11. Don't chew or suck on jewelry made from seeds or beans.
12. Store bulbs and seeds where small children cannot reach them.

Even though you follow these rules, accidents can still happen. To be prepared for emergencies, call Information today and ask for your Poison Control Center's 24-hour hot-line number. Keep the number near the telephone. You may also write to the National Poison Center Network, 125 De Soto Street, Pittsburgh, PA 15213, for the location and telephone number of the center nearest you.

Always keep a bottle of syrup of ipecac at home. (It can be purchased at any drugstore.) Your Poison Control Center or your doctor will tell you how to use it, if necessary.

If you or someone you know eats a plant that may be poisonous, follow these rules:

1. Call your local Poison Control Center *immediately*. You will be asked to give the age and weight of the person who has been poisoned, the person's symptoms, the name of the plant that has been eaten (give the plant's scientific name if you can), and how much of it has been eaten.
2. Follow the instructions the people at the Poison Control Center give you.
3. You may have to rush the victim to the hospital. Call 911 or the police for help in getting an ambulance.
4. Bring any uneaten parts of the plant with you to the hospital or doctor's office.
5. Stay calm! Most cases of plant poisoning are mild and can be cured quickly.

By now, you have learned that poisonous plants grow all around us. Some of them are the source of life saving drugs, while others are prized for their beauty. Some of them give us lovely flowers, shade, and even food. Don't be frightened by the warnings given in this book. Instead, learn as much as you can about the plants around you so that you can enjoy them while remaining safe and healthy. As the poet John Lyly once wrote, "Danger and delight grow on one stalk."

FOR FURTHER READING

Eshleman, Alan. *Poison Plants*. Boston: Houghton Mifflin Company, 1977.

James, Wilma Roberts. *Know Your Poisonous Plants*. Happy Camp, California: Naturegraph Publishers, Inc., 1973.

Lerner, Carol. *Moonseed and Mistletoe*. New York: William Morrow & Co. Inc., 1988.

Levy, Charles Kingsley, and Richard B. Primack. *A Field Guide to Poisonous Plants and Mushrooms of North America*. Brattleboro, Vermont: The Stephen Greene Press, 1984.

Reader's Digest Association. *Magic and Medicine of Plants*. Pleasantville, New York: The Reader's Digest Association, Inc., 1986.

Woodward, Lucia. *Poisonous Plants: A Color Field Guide*. New York: Hippocrene Books, Inc., 1985.

INDEX

ABOUT THE AUTHOR

Since the age of fourteen, when she went to work as a part-time newspaper reporter and columnist, Suzanne M. Coil has been devoted to writing and books. She worked for many years in book publishing in New York, and has also taught writing to college students. Her books for young readers include *George Washington Carver*, *Florida*, and *The Poor in America*. She is currently working on a biography of Harriet Beecher Stowe for young adults. Ms. Coil and her husband, Jesse, live in Covington, Louisiana.